BIEBER
FEVER

KATY SPRINKEL

TRIUMPH
BOOKS

TRIUMPHBOOKS.COM

This book is available in quantity at special discounts for your group or organization. For further information, contact:

Triumph Books
542 South Dearborn Street
Suite 750
Chicago, Illinois 60605
(312) 939-3330
Fax (312) 663-3557
www.triumphbooks.com

Printed in U.S.A.

ISBN: 978-1-60078-664-8

Content developed and packaged by Rockett Media, Inc.
Writer: Katy Sprinkel
Editor: Bob Baker
Design and page production: Andrew Burwell and Paul Petrowsky
Cover design by Paul Petrowsky

Front cover photo courtesy of AP Images
Photographs courtesy of Getty Images unless otherwise noted

CONTENTS

BIEBER

FEVER

CHAPTER 1:

FROM INTERNET SINGER TO
INTERNATIONAL SENSATION

CHAPTER 1:
FROM INTERNET SINGER TO
INTERNATIONAL SENSATION

Justin Bieber was an ordinary 12-year-old Canadian who loved hockey, maple syrup, and Caramilk bars. He played center forward on his local hockey team in Stratford, Ontario. A good student, he counted English class among his favorite subjects. When he wasn't hitting a puck, he was skateboarding, playing basketball, or golfing with his friends.

But there was something special about this "normal" kid. A music lover, Justin had taught himself to play several instruments. It all started innocently with the most modest of things: a bongo drum.

Bieber's concert film *Never Say Never* depicts the auspicious occasion. A young Justin unwraps his Christmas gift, a toy bongo drum. He starts banging on it enthusiastically. His talent is immediately apparent.

Bieber **never** had a vocal coach, he never had a paid lesson.

Justin was named one of Barbara Walters' "10 Most Fascintating People of 2010."

"Where does this talent come from? Can he play drums?" asked bemused neighbor Nathan MacKay. "Man, you gotta get this kid a kit!" And so it went. Justin listened to the music on the radio and tried to mimic the rhythms he heard. He was getting good—really good.

Bieber never had a vocal coach. He never had a paid lesson. "Mom couldn't afford lessons for me, but I knew what I wanted the music to sound like. I could feel it when the chords and melody fit together, the same way you can feel it when your shoes are on the wrong feet," Justin wrote in his autobiography, *First Step 2 Forever.*

Everything he did was by instinct. Those instincts paid off when, in 2007, he entered a local talent contest called Stratford Star. It was a singing contest based roughly on the model of *American Idol.* Many of the contestants were well-trained music students. But it was the doe-eyed, self-taught charmer named Justin Bieber who caught people's attention. He advanced all the way to the finale and was voted runner-up in the competition.

Excited about the triumph, Justin and his mom decided to post a few of the videos of him performing on YouTube so that they could share them with friends and family. Little did they know, clips of "kidrahul," Bieber's YouTube alias, would soon catch fire.

His range and eclectic taste in music was impressive. He tackled everything from Aretha Frankin's "Respect" and Alicia Keys'

"Justin Singing 'With You' by Chris Brown"
was the video that solidified his record deal
and launched his career.

YOUTUBE:
WHERE IT ALL BEGAN

"Justin Singing 'So Sick' by Ne-Yo"

Posted January 19, 2007

The first video Pattie Mallette posted of her son, Justin, was his cover of R&B crooner Ne-Yo's ballad "So Sick." The performance brought the house down at Stratford Star, the talent competition in which Bieber finished second.

"Justin Singing 'Basketball' by Lil Bow Wow"

Posted January 19, 2007

In another jubilant performance from Stratford Star, Justin shows off both his dance moves and his rap skills. The result is wildly entertaining.

"Justin Singing 'Angel' by Sarah McLachlan"

Posted January 20, 2007

Justin did justice to fellow Canadian Sarah McLachlan's haunting ballad. His rendition is imbued with a sensitivity far beyond his years.

"Justin Singing 'Respect' by Aretha Franklin"

Posted January 29, 2007

Justin's soulful cover of "Respect" was the video that made Scooter Braun sit up and take notice.

"Justin Singing in the Bathroom – 'Back at One' by Brian McKnight"

Posted April 25, 2007

Pattie caught her son singing while he was brushing his teeth and committed this one to film. Over 8 million people have seen Bieber's version of the soul classic since it was posted.

"Justin Singing 'I'll Be' by Edwin McCain"

Posted June 5, 2007

Justin breaks out the guitar for the first time online in this gorgeous version of "I'll Be."

"Justin Singing 'Wait for You' by Elliott Yamin"

Posted September 7, 2007

Justin pays homage to another artist who got his start in an unconventional way: American Idol crooner Elliott Yamin.

"Fallin'" to Bow Wow's "Basketball" and Sarah McLachlan's "Angel." People were watching…and watching…and waiting for more Justin. One of those people was Scott Samuel "Scooter" Braun, a party promoter–turned–talent manager from Atlanta.

Two weeks later, Bieber and his mom were in Georgia, inking a talent deal with Braun. They spent months adding clips to the YouTube page, increasing viewership on Justin's channel even more. His cover of Chris Brown's "With You" hit 1 million views after just one month. And that's when Justin Timberlake and Usher both sat up and took notice. One of the music moguls was going to book this kid.

"I felt like his voice was incredible. I felt he was very charismatic and that's what it takes to be able to handle what this is. It's the ability to turn it on and understand, but it was a very real ability. It was actually just him," Usher told MTV News about first

Bieber's YouTube views have eclipsed 1 billion.

hearing Bieber sing. "But also just his musical talent—the fact that he taught himself to play guitar, the fact that he taught himself to play piano to the point where he can write and create his own songs. [I said to him,] 'You're a prodigy.'"

In April 2008 Usher and super-producer L.A. Reid signed Justin to Island Def Jam. The rest, as they say, is history.

Bieber's debut album, *My World*, went certified platinum, with five songs charting on the Billboard Hot 100 list including "One Less Lonely Girl," "Love Me," and "My Favorite Girl." He followed up with *My World 2.0*, an expanded edition of his first album that included collaborations with Ludacris (the smash hit "Baby") and Sean Kingston ("Eenie Meenie"). His mentor Usher even got in on the act, dueting with the young singer on "Somebody to Love."

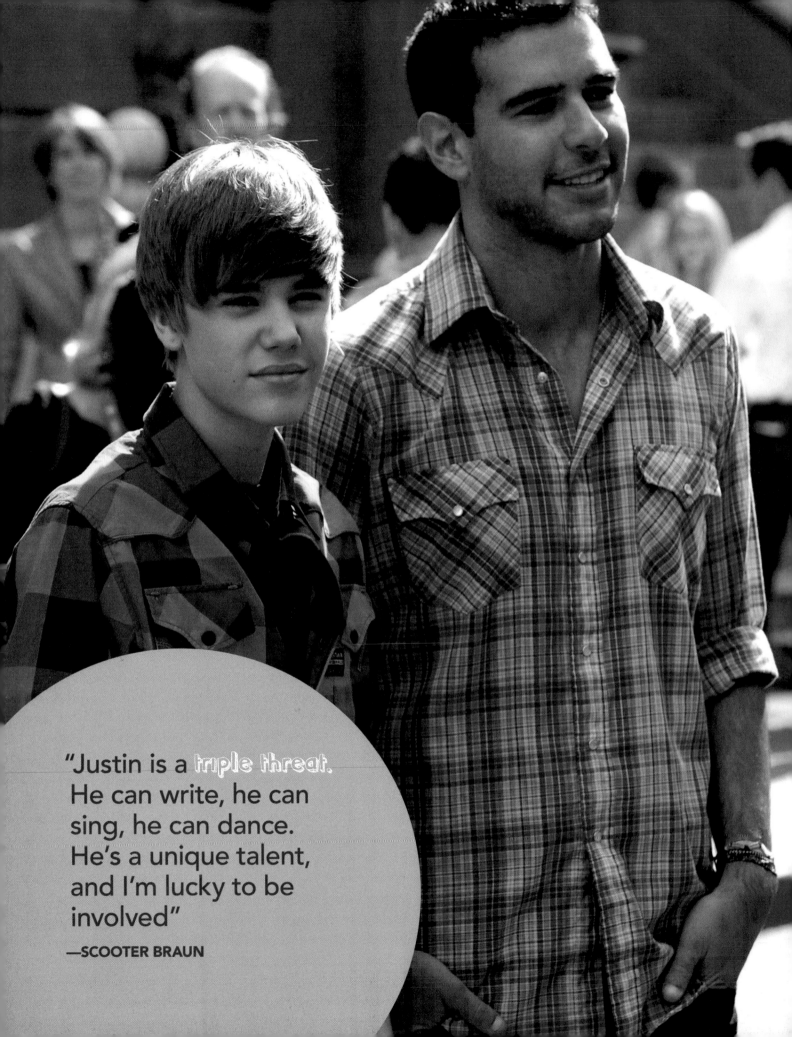

"Justin is a triple threat. He can write, he can sing, he can dance. He's a unique talent, and I'm lucky to be involved"

—SCOOTER BRAUN

WHO IS SCOOTER BRAUN?

→**WHAT WAS BRAUN'S REACTION WHEN HE FIRST SAW JUSTIN'S VIDEOS?** "I heard the tone in his voice and I saw some instrumentation and it was just raw talent. And my gut went crazy," Braun told the *Hollywood Reporter.* "I became completely obsessed with tracking him down."

→**WHEN SCOOTER BRAUN CAME CALLING AFTER SEEING JUSTIN'S YOUTUBE PAGE, HE DIDN'T HAVE MUCH LUCK FINDING HIM.** He searched through photo archives of the theater where Justin performed in Stratford Star, but to no avail. He made several pleading phone calls to Bieber's school in Stratford before finally convincing them to pass on the message—and then Pattie Mallette didn't even call him back! Once the two did talk, it took a lot of convincing to win her over.

→**BRAUN'S FIRST CAREER EVOLVED OUT OF HIS PASSION FOR PLANNING PARTIES,** something he did regularly as an undergraduate at Emory University. His big break into the music business came in 2002, as a sophomore in college, when he was hired to plan parties for Ludacris and Eminem. Braun left college to become executive director of marketing for Jermaine Dupri's So Def record label at the age of 20.

→**BRAUN ALWAYS HAD AN EYE FOR TALENT.** He signed rapper Asher Roth—who went on to become a Billboard-charting artist for his debut album *Asleep in the Bread Aisle*—and embarked on a new career as a talent manager.

His newest release, *Never Say Never - The Remixes*, was also a No. 1 album.

But the real measure of success hasn't just been on the charts. Justin's *My World* world tour has been a towering success. He played to sold-out crowds across the U.S. and Canada in 2010 and on the international leg of his tour in early 2011.

He won four trophies at the American Music Awards, taking home top honors for Artist of the Year, Favorite Pop/Rock Male Artist, Favorite Pop/Rock Album (for *My World 2.0*), and Breakthrough Artist. He also has a BET Award, three Teen Choice Awards, a VMA, and a couple of MuchMusic Awards to his credit. And he shows no signs of stopping.

But if you ask Bieber, 2011 is shaping up to be even bigger. With the tour continuing abroad, a successful movie behind him, and several business ventures in progress, it looks like everything's coming up Justin. "As far as music and entertainment, that's the beginning," Usher said of his protégé to MTV News. The teenager is poised for an incredible year in an already amazing career.

ATTENTION WORLD:
Prepare for total Bieber domination!

BIEBER

FEVER

CHAPTER 2:

NEVER SAY NEVER

CHAPTER 2:
NEVER SAY NEVER

February 11 marked Justin Bieber's big-screen debut: the world premiere of his biopic and concert film, *Never Say Never*. The film charts Bieber's meteoric rise to fame, culminating in a sold-out performance at New York's Madison Square Garden.

This up-close-and-personal look at the singer—his life on the road, backstage, and in the spotlight—also features exclusive home movies of Justin's childhood, chronicling his earliest musical moments. The videos offer further proof of the musician's prodigious talents, giving viewers a privileged glimpse of the birth of a star.

The concert footage—all recorded during the August 31, 2010, stop in New York—offers something even better: front-row seats to one of Bieber's most explosive performances, all in 3-D. Theatergoers received special 3-D "sunglasses" in Justin's favorite color, purple, of course! Special guest stars at the concert included Miley Cyrus, Ludacris, Usher, Sean Kingston, Jaden Smith, and Bieber's idols, Boyz II Men.

*Never Say Never is the **ultimate** valentine to Bieber fans, whom the singer calls "the greatest fans in the world."*

JUSTIN TAKES HOLLYWOOD

Never Say Never may be his first time appearing on the silver screen, but Justin is no stranger to acting.

He made his small-screen debut in an episode of CBS's hit drama *CSI: Crime Scene Investigation* in Septem-

Hollywood insiders have also reported that Justin is the top choice to replace Ashton Kutcher in a reboot of the MTV prank series *Punk'd.*

ber 2010. In the episode, he plays a character with a dark side who finds himself in the crosshairs of Las Vegas' forensic investigators. The episode ended with him behind bars—and in big trouble.

He also appeared on *Saturday Night Live,* on which he was booked as the show's musical guest. The pop star gamely acted in one sketch in which he played a charming student whose teacher, played by Tina Fey, is quite age-inappropriately enchanted by his boyish good looks.

Hollywood insiders have also reported that Justin is the top choice to replace Ashton Kutcher in a reboot of the MTV prank series *Punk'd.* Those who know Justin well know that he is notoriously goofy, so it seems a logical fit. Whether or not there's any truth to the casting report is unclear; representatives in Bieber's camp have not yet commented.

There's no doubt that there is more acting in Justin's future. He's already been linked to several big-screen projects…

"Honestly, it was the best thing I've ever been to in my life," said one fan lucky enough to attend the show. Another fan added, "He danced, he sang, he played piano, drums, guitar, and he was just so cute!"

"[Bieber] is a bona fide teen-pop dreamboat in an otherwise barren post-Jonas Brothers era, and a young dynamo who's essentially self-made, not just affiliated with the Disney or Nickelodeon star-making machines," wrote the *New York Times*.

Singer Bow Wow (left) and actress Jessica Jarrell were just two of the friends Justin greeted at *Variety's* fourth annual Power of Youth event.

JUSTIN
AT THE MOVIES

It's little surprise that the boy who came from humble beginnings, worked hard to get noticed, and achieved greatness under incredible odds gravitates to a movie hero who did the very same thing. *Rocky* is the story of an unknown boxer from Philadelphia, Rocky Balboa, who gets the chance of a lifetime to fight the heavyweight champion of the world, Apollo Creed. Creed is expected to win the fight, but Rocky is determined to go the distance against the champ.

Like its main character, *Rocky* was a box-office smash, and it won the Academy Award for Best Picture in 1977.

There's another movie hero Justin appreciates: Chuck Norris. Norris got

his start as a martial artist. He broke into Hollywood in the early 1970s and became a well-known action star in the '80s and later a television success as star of *Walker: Texas Ranger*.

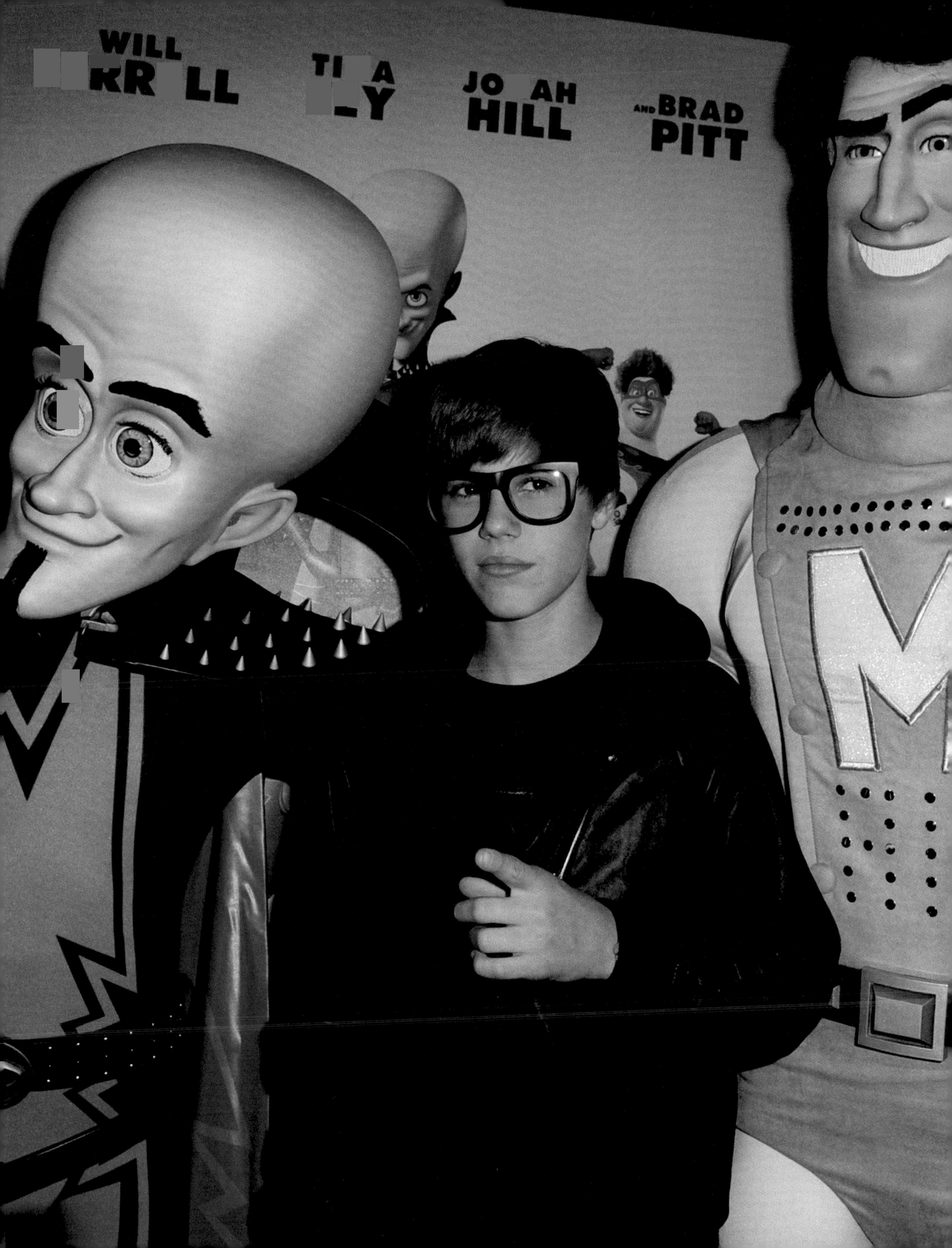
WILL
HILL
AND BRAD
PITT

Justin interviews Jeremy Renner at the 16th annual Critics Choice Awards

"He showed himself to be a direct heir of two-plus decades of uptempo R&B, spanning from Michael Jackson to New Jack Swing to Auto-Tune, streamlined for pop ears," wrote the *New York Times*.

"Don't believe dreams come true? Think about this—I'm [followed by] more people on Twitter than live in my entire hometown. Dreams *do* come true," he Tweeted to his followers.

"My dreams used to be a one-in-a-million chance…but as I said in the song, never say never," he wrote in *First Step 2 Forever*.

The movie takes its title from the single of the same name, a collaboration that he worked on with Jaden Smith, the son of former rapper and movie star Will Smith and an actor in his own right. The song "Never Say Never" appeared in 2009's *The Karate Kid*, in which Jaden played the title role. After working on the song and video together, Justin described Jaden, three years younger than him, as his "li'l bro."

Nothing could sum up his success better than these lyrics from the song: "Gonna give everything I have/It's my destiny."

Justin Bieber and Maria Menounos attend the *Access Hollywood* 'Stuff You Must...' Lounge.

BIEBER

FEVER

CHAPTER 3:

UNDER THE **INFLUENCE**

CHAPTER 3:
UNDER THE INFLUENCE

As the movie *Never Say Never* documents, Justin was exposed to a lot of music early on in his life. It's little surprise that his musical influences range from Stevie Wonder to Destiny's Child to Guns N' Roses. It seems the radio was always on in the house—or somebody was making music.

Pattie recognized Justin's need for a real drum set but couldn't afford one, so her musician friends scheduled a local gig to raise money for her son's instrument. And it worked: the musicians earned enough to get Justin his own kit, complete with kick and snare drums, floor toms, cymbals, and a hi-hat.

The church that Justin attended had a large contemporary praise band. Early on, he wanted in on the action, and soon, members of the band were letting little Justin bang on the drums and piano. It became evident to them, too, that he could play.

But drumming was only the beginning. As soon as he was able to get his arms around a guitar, he started strum-

◀ Paula Abdul, Justin Bieber, and Usher arrive at Nickelodeon's 2009 Kids' Choice Awards.

▶ Justin Bieber and Usher pose for a portrait during the 2010 American Music Awards.

Beyonce and Justin in the audience during the 52nd Annual GRAMMY Awards.

JUSTIN'S
FIRST BRUSH WITH FAME

Usher and Justin pose in the audience at the 2010 American Music Awards.

Justin remembers 2001, which he calls "a very good year for music. It was the year that Destiny's Child put out "Survivor" and "Bootylicious," which first alerted the singer to his idol and celebrity crush Beyonce. It was also the year that Usher released his No. 1 Billboard hit "U Remind Me."

On the day that Justin and his mom flew to Atlanta to meet with manager Scooter Braun, they had an immediate brush with fame, encountering Usher in the parking lot of Braun's office. Justin was immediately starstruck, but felt he couldn't let the moment pass without approaching his idol. He tried to persuade the recording artist to listen to his vocals, but the singer politely refused. Justin was disappointed, but the chance encounter steeled his resolve. He was going to be a star.

As it turns out, Justin didn't have to wait long to get a second chance with Usher. The two met again just six months later, and Usher moved fast to close the deal. And from that moment on, Justin's world changed forever. *My World* would soon follow.

"I'm definitely influenced by Michael Jackson and Boyz II Men and other black artists. That's what I like."

ming. His father taught him some Bob Dylan songs like "Knockin' on Heaven's Door," and the world of rock 'n' roll opened up to Justin. First it was Dylan, then Aerosmith, Jimi Hendrix, and Van Halen. "[Dad] taught me how to play barre chords…[and] if you know the basic form of five or six barre chords, you can play any song in the universe," Justin wrote in *First Step 2 Forever.*

But the predominant music that Justin enjoyed was always R&B. "Michael Jackson is an icon to me. I want to be a great entertainer like him," he told *Women's Wear Daily.*

"I'm definitely influenced by Michael Jackson and Boyz II Men and other black artists. That's what I like. But I like their voices and I like how they entertain—it's not about what color they are." he told *Vanity Fair.*

He credits Boyz II Men with inspiring him vocally and performed onstage with his idols at Madison Square Garden.

Justin has certainly taken cues from the King of Pop, who is remembered as an all-around entertainer and one of the greatest dancers of all time. Justin's live performances are far

from him standing center stage and belting it out to the audience. It's a full-contact sport, and he commands the stage with his infectious energy.

His dance moves are inspired by Jackson and another famous dancer close to the performer's heart: Usher. Bieber's steps are the creation of choreographer Jamaica Craft, who ensures that every moment of Justin's 75-minute set is pure entertainment. It's not just about the music, it's about the total package. "A lot of hard work goes into performing," Bieber wrote in *First Step 2 Forever.* Indeed, leading up to the *My World* tour, Justin was practicing his dance moves 12 hours a day!

But for all the musical influences, Justin is steadfast about remaining true to who he is. "I've never tried to sound like anybody,"

Rihanna and Justin attend the Island Def Jam
Spring Collection party.

He also points to artists like Beyonce, Justin Timberlake, Lil Wayne, Green Day, Tupac, Blink-182, and Bob Dylan as influences. It might sound like an eclectic mixture, but Justin doesn't see it that way. "Music is the universal language no

---

Justin has had the chance to work alongside some of his greatest music heroes and inspirations.

---

matter the country we are born in or the color of our skin. Brings us all together," he once Tweeted.

But for all the musical influences, Justin is steadfast about remaining true to who he is. "I've never tried to sound like anybody," he told *McLean's* magazine. He's said that the worst thing he could hear about himself is to be described as a carbon copy of another artist. Luckily, Justin's talents speak for themselves. He is every bit a genuine artist and true to his own instincts.

FAREWELL
TO THE KING

Justin's single "One Time" was climbing the charts when a bolt from the blue arrived: the singer's idol, Michael Jackson, suddenly died. Justin took the news hard.

"I was devastated. One of my greatest idols, and my inspiration, was gone," he wrote in *First Step 2 Forever*.

Jackson's imitable stage presence has been a huge influence on how Justin models his stage shows. But the artist has also been an inspiration for Justin's music. Justin even modeled the song "Pray," which he cowrote with Omar Martinez and Adam Messinger and Nasri Atweh of the Messengers, after Jackson's inspirational song "Man in the Mirror."

"I definitely thought of Michael [Jackson's] 'Man in the Mirror' when I was writing it." "There's so many songs about love and I think that it's great to take it out of that world for a minute. There's [sic] other things that are important and I just wanted to be motivational," he told Ryan Seacrest in a radio interview.

Justin has incorporated a tribute to the late artist into his stage shows on the My World tour, which he describes as a "good reminder for me about what matters in the business." When introducing his backup band and dance crew by name, the strains of Jackson's "Wanna Be Startin' Something" play in the background.

BIEBER

FEVER

CHAPTER 4:

KEEPING UP WITH KIM
AND OTHER FAMOUS FRIENDS

KEEPING UP WITH KIM
AND OTHER FAMOUS FRIENDS

Justin made headlines when photographs first surfaced of him and Kim Kardashian posing on a beach together. As it turned out, the duo was shooting a photo spread for *Elle* magazine.

But the photographs caused a huge uproar among the media and Bieber Nation alike. Bill O'Reilly, conservative journalist and host of *The O'Reilly Factor*, spoke out about the photographs, describing the age difference between

Hail to the Chief

If meeting Beyonce was enough to make the star nervous, then meeting the President of the United States was terrifying. Bieber was asked to join a distinguished group of musicians—including Mary J. Blige, Sugarland, Neil Diamond, Rob Thomas, and Usher—to perform holiday music at the White House for a program called Christmas in Washington.

His performance went off great—with one hitch. When President Obama introduced the singer, he mispronounced his last name "BYE-ber." BEE-ber was of course forgiving of the blunder.

"He messed up my name, but I gave it to him. He's not [the] age category I sing to," Justin told *People* magazine.

Obama's daughters, Sasha and Malia, are a different story. Both girls are big fans. "[I] met them, took pictures with them, took pictures with the First Lady," Justin told MTV News of his first visit. Since then, he has twice been invited back to the White House to perform.

And you can bet the President definitely knows how to pronounce his name by now. In a recent interview on *The View*, President Obama gushed about the singer, saying, "I have met Justin Bieber. He came to sing at the White House. He's a very nice young man."

Taylor Swift and Justin attend Z100's Jingle Ball 2009.

the 29-year-old starlet and 16-year-old singer as inappropriate.

Some fans were no less forgiving. There were even overzealous protestors who took to Kardashian's Twitter page and left her threatening messages. "I was getting the craziest messages from all of the Beliebers," Kardashian told *US* magazine. "And so I was Twittering him, like 'Hey Bliebs, this is crazy, getting death threats from your fans.' I think they were 10-year-olds who got carried away, so he asked all of his Beliebers to stop attacking me."

Ringo Starr, Justin, and Ke$ha during the dress rehearsal at Staples Center.

The two became friends after first meeting at the 2010 White House Correspondents' Dinner. But as they both will readily admit, just friends is as far as it goes with them.

Of course, Justin is first and foremost a musician, so he's often seen in the company of fellow recording artists from Atlanta. He worked with fellow labelmate Ludacris on a version of the single "Baby." The rapper recalled first meeting Justin in an interview with MTV News. "When I first met Justin, man, I felt like he's definitely a little shy at first. I understand. I'm kind of the same way till I get comfortable with my surroundings, and then it's just all out, just wild. Oh man, his career is just starting. When I tell you the longevity—he's out of here."

Justin also became fast friends with Taylor Swift after joining her as a performer on her tour of the United Kingdom. The two regularly exchange messages via Twitter, often sending each other congratulations on accolades

that they've received. Both young singers are also established songwriters. Can a duet between the buddies be far behind?

Hollywood life is certainly agreeing with Justin. He recently appeared at the Golden Globes, where he was scheduled as a presenter. When asked whom he met at the ceremony, he commented with a sly grin, "I met Angelina Jolie."

Jolie's costar in *The Tourist*, Johnny Depp, also on hand for the awards, had previously met the singer. According to the New York Post, Depp brought his two children, Lily Rose and Jack, to a performance Bieber gave in Florida and they visited backstage before the show. At one point in the performance, Justin looked out over the crowd and asked playfully, "What do you think Johnny Depp would want me to play?"

But for all the time in the limelight, Justin remains close with his two best friends from Stratford, Ryan Butler and Chaz Somers. The three were hockey teammates back in Ontario, and have remained close even after Justin relocated to Atlanta, and embarked on a world tour.

Russell Brand, Justin, and Katy Perry attend the 2010 American Music Awards.

Justin and Selena
It's On!

Justin and Selena Gomez have known each other for a while, but the two singers took some time to acknowledge that their friendship might well be a romance. When photographs surfaced depicting the pair getting cozy in the Caribbean, the Internet went wild with speculation.

"He's been my best friend for a long time," Gomez said in a radio interview with New York's Z100, in which she confirmed the relationship rumors. Bieber has also come clean, telling British magazine *The People*, "She is a really great person and I think she has the best smile in the world."

The Wizards of Waverly Place actress downplayed the talk. "We just like to hang out.

They shouldn't be stopping us from going out to dinner and things like that," she told *People* magazine.

Bieber seconded the assertion, telling *MTV News* of Gomez, "She's really cool. She's an amazing person." But he added: "I gotta keep some things to myself. I'm having fun just being a teenager."

When the pair showed up together to make the rounds at the post-Oscar parties—wearing matching outfits, no less—the couple finally took their romance public.

The teenage romance hasn't been all hearts and flowers (Selena even received death threats from overzealous JB fans), but the couple is still going strong.

What will be the couple's moniker? Will it be Selieber? Justomez? Bieberena? Your guess is as good as ours...

BIEBER

FEVER

CHAPTER 5:

JUSTIN GETS **TWITTER-PATED**

CHAPTER 5:

JUSTIN GETS
TWITTER-PATED

In 2010, Justin was named the most influential Twitter celebrity. He received this award for good reason. His Twitter feed, www.twitter.com/justinbieber, has more than 7 million

followers and accounts for 3 percent of the website's total bandwidth.

It could be said that he is setting the new model for social networking. His Twitter reads like an insider's guide to all things Bieber. Followers are the first to preview new material, getting the early scoop on film trailers, posters, forthcoming singles, and music videos.

Perhaps as important, followers get an inside look at the mind of Justin Bieber. He has made a special effort to check in often from the road, and his Tweets read like the singer's tour diary.

A look at some of Justin's Tweets show how introspective the young singer is about his life so far.

> → i think i understand im not living a normal life anymore...but im normal. people say all sorts of stuff but i know who i am and im grateful
> 11:44 PM Jan 18th via web

> → i want to make #newmusic and share it with all of u.
> 5:01 PM Dec 31st, 2010 via web

Justin and his mother Pattie Mallette visit the *Late Show with David Letterman* at the Ed Sullivan Theater.

Kanye West performs onstage at The Cosmopolitan Grand Opening and New Year's Eve Celebration.

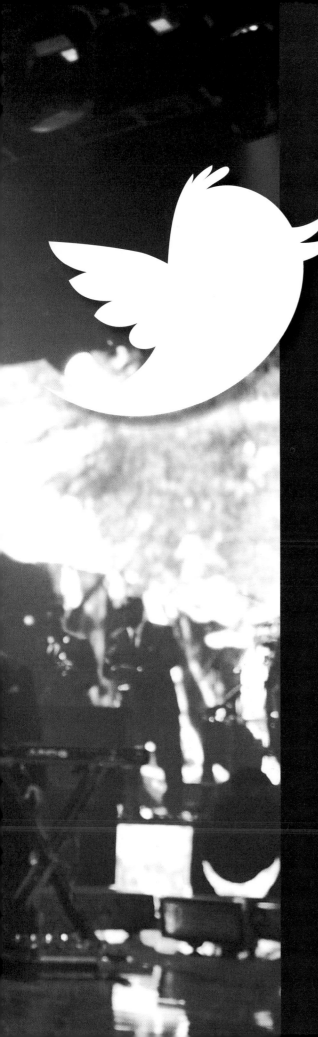

Kanye
Tweets Justin

It all started innocently, when uber-Tweeter Kanye West sent this post to his Twitter followers:

"Listening to Justin Bieber 'Run Away Love'... I love Sunday mornings in the crib." "Can't blame Yeezy, that song is the jam"

West quickly followed the Tweet with another: "I just did the most cliche celebrity tweet of all time... listening to! When people tweet that I'm always like... uuum great .. so what!"

Through the power of Twitter, Justin caught wind of West's praise and responded in kind.

"It's not a so what moment for me," he responded. "I'm 16 and a fan. I'm kinda hyped u are listening to my stuff. Thank u. Nice sunday morning."

"And I'm honored that you like my Music @JustinBieber!!! You gotta hear the album. Maybe we can do something together. Me, You, and Raekwon," he continued.
And from that exchange, a collaboration was born. Just two weeks later Kanye West's remix of "Runaway Love" featuring Raekwon—of the Wu-Tang Clan—and Justin Bieber was completed. The song was a huge success for all three artists and a strong testament to the power of social networking—or more specifically, in this case, microblogging.

→ so my #newyearsresolution is to continue to give back for my blessings and do more than the year before. i wanna #makeachange
5:01 PM Dec 31st, 2010 via web

→ #2011 the dream...would be to win a grammy. that would be just amazing. a boy can dream right? #2011
4:05 PM Dec 31st, 2010 via web

→ all people are equal and all people deserve respect. but with the respect the lord teaches forgiveness. a new year is coming. let him judge
5:15 PM Dec 30th, 2010 via web

He frequently takes the time to show his fans his gratitude, writing:

→ That is how u end a tour!! Felt incredible. So grateful and still can't believe it. #myworldtour
11:20 PM Dec 23rd, 2010 via ÜberTwitter

→ I had to kill em and bring out @akon and @LUDACRIS -- ATL we killed em tonight!! #SWAG
11:19 PM Dec 23rd, 2010 via ÜberTwitter

→ Tonight my dude @seankingston surprised me with @bowwow and @ souljaboy then...
11:18 PM Dec 23rd, 2010 via ÜberTwitter

→ 4 years ago I started this account www.youtube.com/kidrauhl - thanks for taking this ride with me. #wearejustgettingstarted #neversaynever
1:13 PM Jan 16th via web

He also realizes the power of social networking, giving fans a first look at what's coming ahead.

→ u dont have to be a fan to see the movie. you dont have to like the music. you just have to want to see a great movie. thanks @jonmchu
Wednesday, January 19, 2011 12:05:05 PM via web

Justin and rock legend Ozzy Osbourne pose on the set of Best Buy's inaugural Big Game commercial.

CHAPTER 5: JUSTIN GETS **TWITTER-PATED**

Tour Diary

→ everyone asks me what im doing... im a teenager..im doing school.
May 16, 2011 via web

→ dedicated #PRAY to the people of Japan tonight and the OLLG was one of the students i met yesterday. Really special night and a great show.
May 19th via web

→ sometimes its cool to just sit back and watch the videos on www.youtube.com/kidrauhl — come a long way since stratford idol. #grateful
April 30th via web

Thanks to Fans

→ just met some incredible kids who have been thru alot because of the devastation here in Japan. blessed to meet them and proud to know them
May 18th via web

→ and thank u to all of u seeing #NSN3Daround the world! getting notes from France, S. Africa, UK, Brazil, Argentina..and many more!r
Mar 16th via web

→ 8 MILLION of THE GREATEST FANS ON EARTH!!! THANK U. LOVE U. NEVER SAY NEVER.
Mar 9th via web

Humor

→ Indonesia was HYPED!!! Great show and met the Indonesian CHUCK NORRIS...he was the guy driving the pickup truck in our Police escort.
April 23rd via web

→ WHAT!?!? Singapore has heated toilet seats!?! @kennyhamilton Score!! This really city from the future! Lol
April 18th via web

→ WHAT!?!? Singapore has heated toilet seats!?! @kennyhamilton Score!! This really city from the future! Lol
April 18th via web

Inspiration

→ dont spread gossip and dont spread rumors about others...im a kid and i know that.
May 9th via web

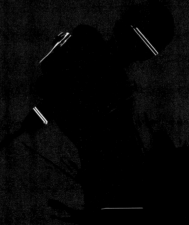

you cant please everyone...
you need to stick up for
yourself...but you can always
be kind
April 11th via web

➜   Someone said to me
tonight its not your suc-
cesses that define u but
your failures.I lost [at the
Grammys]..but I don't
plan on this being my last
chance....
Feb 13th via ÜberSocialOrig

➜   something else i saw
i liked in a book a fan
gave me was B.I.E.B.E.R
= Believe In Everything
Because Everything is
Reachable. love that
Monday, January 03, 2011
12:09:18 PM via web

His Twitter messages
are a testament to his
honesty and approach-
ability, qualities that have
made him the most fol-
lowed personality on the
site. And his numbers
just keep on growing.

BIEBER

FEVER

CHAPTER 6:
BRANDING **JUSTIN BIEBER**

CHAPTER 6:

BRANDING
JUSTIN BIEBER

These days it seems like everyone famous has his or her own signature scent. But leave it to Justin to think outside of the box. The singer has launched a new line of products that combine fashion and scent in one package.

He has joined forces with the company Etoile Nation Beauty to introduce wristbands and dog tags infused with four different scents. (Etoile means "star" in French, the other language that Justin speaks fluently.) The accessories all bear Justin's image and

"You have yet to see the best of Justin Bieber. He's only 16, he's getting better and better,"

—Ne-Yo

Celebrities and Their Fragrances

Paris Hilton has one. So does Eva Longoria. Tim McGraw and Faith Hill each have their own. Britney Spears has four of them.

They're fragrances, and big-name endorsements can translate into big sales. Just check out this list of top earners for 2009, based on research done by Chicago-based independent market researcher Euromonitor International.

America's Best-Selling Celebrity Scents

1. Elizabeth Taylor "White Diamonds" (right)
$67.2 million

2. Sean John "Unforgivable"
$48.5 million

3. Celine Dion
$26.4 million

4. "Lovely" by Sarah Jessica Parker
$25.7 million

5. Derek Jeter "Driven"
$24.1 million

6. "Diavolo" by Antonio Banderas
$18.8 million

7. "Glo" by J.Lo
18.5 million

8. "Curious" by Britney Spears
$14.3 million

9. "Fantasy" by Britney Spears
$10.1 million

CHAPTER 6: BRANDING
JUSTIN BIEBER

feature signature scents called Icon, Energy, Tour, and Web. If it sounds like a laundry list of the factors that have made Justin a household name, it's by design.

Each accessory is infused with the fragrance using a patented resin technology that holds the scent for up to a year. It's easy to see why Justin, on the cutting edge of music as an Internet-grown phenomenon, has embraced the new fragrance technology.

His perfumed accessories line is just the latest in a growing list of merchandise to which he has lent his name. On the singer's website, fans can buy everything from T-shirts and loungewear to calendars and trading cards. He has puzzles and board games, plush bears, iPhone and iPod skins, Christmas stockings, coffee mugs, pins, picture frames, posters, tote bags, and stationery. And that's just the half of it! Fans can even buy Bieber-themed jewelry. He sells personalized bracelets, pendants, and earrings emblazoned with his portrait.

If that's not enough, fans can also get their hands on a series of collectible dolls featuring a pocket-sized Justin sporting some of his most memorable looks from red-carpet and music-video appearances. Each doll plays a snippet of one of Justin's songs, including "Baby," "One Less Lonely Girl," and "Somebody to Love."

He even joined forces with linens company Lady Sandra Home Fashions to launch a personalized line of bedding. So now fans can cozy up to Justin even while they sleep!

He recently teamed with cosmetics company OPI to release a line of nail

$100 million and trailing only New Jersey–born arena rockers Bon Jovi.

Could a line of shoes be next for Justin? "[I'm a] big shoe guy," he told *Women's Wear Daily*, adding that before his fame he couldn't really afford a lot of pairs. "So, now I'm going nuts.

Marketing Justin Bieber has become big business. Published estimates put the singer's net worth at over $5.5 million.

polish shades named after his songs. The first six shades were launched in December and sold out immediately from Wal-Mart, the exclusive retailer.

He has also inked deals with Xbox, Proactiv, and Best Buy. And he appeared in the highest of advertising profiles: a Super Bowl commercial. The ad features Justin in yet another unlikely pairing, this time with hard rocker Ozzy Osbourne.

Marketing Justin Bieber has become big business. Published estimates put the singer's net worth at over $5.5 million. *Forbes* named him one of the top teen celebrity entrepreneurs in 2010. In fact, the *Los Angeles Times* reported that he was the second-highest grossing entertainer of 2010 in album sales and concert revenues, making over

Supras are my favorite. I just like finding shoes no one else has, exclusives. [I] love shoes. [They're] kind of my thing."

The sky's the limit. "You have yet to see the best of Justin Bieber. He's only 16, he's getting better and better," said fellow artist Ne-Yo. "Watch out for that dude."

Bieber's mentor, Usher, seconded the notion when he spoke with MTV News. "As far as music and entertainment, that's the beginning. There's so much more in store for the future, or at least there's a ton of things we can do and will, and with the support of his fans who will continue to just grow and grow and grow."

Justin accepts the T-Mobile Breakthrough Artist of the Year award from singer Natasha Bedingfield.

Justin the Book Author

In October 2010 Justin took a big step in his already huge career when his autobiography, *First Step 2 Forever*, was published. The book was an instant success, surging to the top of the best-seller lists.

The book is a backstage pass into Justin's life, and he shares the milestones of his life and career along the way. It is Justin in his own words, sharing new secrets about what makes him tick and how he keeps sane with such a busy schedule. Through the book, readers can see that despite all the fame and glory, he's still a normal teenager.

Here are a few of the tidbits he reveals in his book:

On family: "If you feel like a freak because you don't have a normal family, I've got news for you: pretty much nobody does. In fact, I don't know if there's such thing as a 'normal family.'"

On losing: "Grandpa told me, 'You can lose without feeling like a loser. If you take the experience and learn from it, you're still coming out ahead of where you were before.'"

On keeping his singing a secret from classmates: "Kids had no idea I did music. Some of them thought it was their job to put me in my place, and I had a sinking feeling this video montage [of his performances, which was played at his school] was going to make them even tougher on me."

On his favorite food: "Singers aren't supposed to have dairy before a show, but we all know I'm a rule breaker. Pizza is just so good!"

On staying normal: "Pranks vs. school = pranks win all day. Can you blame me? I'm just a kid."

BIEBER

FEVER

CHAPTER 7:
JUSTIN **GIVES BACK**

Michael Jackson sang, danced, wrote music, and was the quintessential performer. But he left an indelible impression on Justin Bieber for an altogether different reason.

"Michael Jackson was the most giving artist of all time," Justin wrote in *First Step 2 Forever*. "If I can do just one-tenth of the good he did for others, I can really make a difference in this world. That's what it's all about."

In January 2010 a massive earthquake struck the island of Haiti, causing widespread destruction and claiming more than 300,000 lives. The world grieved, and people around the world began efforts to rebuild the country, donating relief funds to the Red Cross and other organizations to get help to the devastated country.

Twenty-five years earlier, a group of recording artists grieved for another

Ella Rae Wahlberg and Justin attend *Variety*'s 4th annual Power of Youth event at Paramount Studios.

Justin performs at the 'We Are The World 25 Years for Haiti' recording session held at Jim Henson Studios.

(L-R) Singers Gladys Knight, Celine Dion, Joe Jonas, Kevin Jonas, and Justin Bieber perform at the 'We Are The World 25 Years for Haiti' recording session held at Jim Henson Studios.

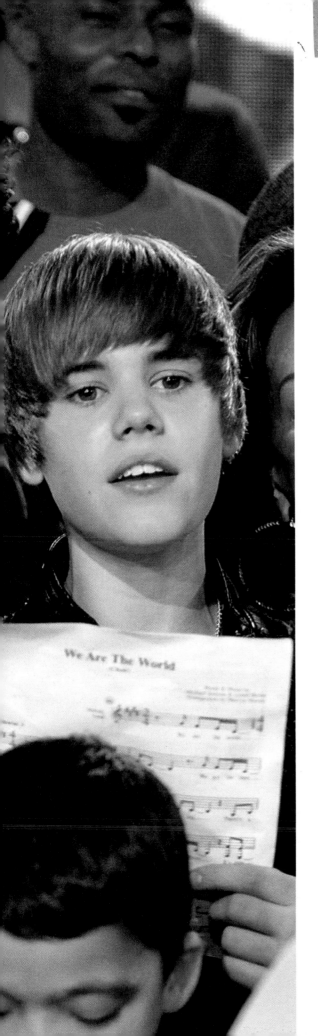

We Are the World

The 25th anniversary version of "We Are the World" to aid Haiti was executive produced by original producer Quincy Jones, cowriter Lionel Richie, and Haiti native Wyclef Jean. **Here's a full listing of the participants.**

Akon • India.Arie • Patti Austin • Farnsworth Bentley Tony Bennett • Justin Bieber • Bone Thugs-n-Harmony (Bizzy Bones) • Mary J. Blige • Ethan Bortnick Brandy • Toni Braxton • Jeff Bridges • Zac Brown Natalie Cole • Harry Connick Jr. • Nikka Costa Miley Cyrus • Celine Dion • Drake • Earth Wind & Fire Faith Evans • Fergie • Melanie Fiona • Jamie Foxx Sean Garrett • Tyrese Gibson • Josh Groban Anthony Hamilton • Keith Harris • Heart • Keri Hilson Julianne Hough • Jennifer Hudson • Enrique Iglesias Il Trio • Iyaz • Randy Jackson • Taj Jackson Taryll Jackson • TJ Jackson • Al Jardine • Wyclef Jean The Jonas Brothers • Quincy Jones • Rashida Jones Kid Cudi • Gladys Knight • Adam Levine • Lil Wayne LL Cool J • Jimmy Jean Louis • Joel & Benji Madden Mann • Mary Mary • Katharine McPhee • Rickey Minor Jason Mraz • Musiq SoulchildMya • Nipsey Hussle Orianthi • Freda Payne • P!nk • Plain Pat • Ar Rahmen RedOne • Lionel Richie • Nicole Richie • Raphael Saadiq Carlos Santana • Nicole Scherzinger • Isaac Slade (a.k.a. the Fray) • Snoop Dogg • Trey Songz Jordin Sparks • Barbra Streisand • Sugarland Robin Thicke • Rob Thomas • T Pain • Usher Vince Vaughn • Kanye West • will.i.am Brian Wilson • Bebe Winans

Justin poses with the gold disc at his fan event at La Qua Garden amusement park.

tragedy. People in Ethopia were literally starving to death, the victims of a crippling famine. Recording artists Michael Jackson and Lionel Richie wrote the song "We Are the World" and,

Jones said in a statement about the new production, "25 years ago, the entertainment industry showed the power of community to help our fellow man when we recorded 'We Are the

Justin was one of the more the 80 artists who felt the call to action to help Haiti, including singers from Wyclef Jean, Kanye West, Mary J. Blige, and Drake to Sugarland, Julianne Hough, Miley Cyrus, and Josh Groban

along with producers Quincy Jones and Michael Omartian, established USA for Africa in an effort to bring relief to the country. Together, they rallied 47 top singers to record the song for charity. The song was honored with numerous awards and accolades and eventually became the top-selling single of all time. To date, proceeds from the song have raised more than $65 million in relief funds for sub-Saharan Africa.

When the earthquake hit Haiti in 2010, the men behind the original "We Are the World" recording were inspired to revive the song, this time with a new purpose.

World' to bring relief to those suffering from famine in Ethiopia. And while the need to assist Africa continues, today the country of Haiti is suffering immeasurably from the destruction due to the recent earthquake and is in immediate need of relief that will last long after the television cameras have left. As artists, we have joined together on this 25th anniversary and in the spirit of 'We Are the World' to help meet that need."

Justin was one of the more than 80 artists who felt the call to action to help Haiti. "'We Are the World' was incredible," Justin told *MTV News*. "I got to work with...all the greats.... It

Justin at the 2010 MTV Video Music Awards.

Justin "Prays" for Change

Justin started out as an acoustic singer, busking on the streets of Stratford and strumming his guitar in videos he posted to YouTube. With his album *My Worlds Acoustic* he joined the likes of Mariah Carey, Eric Clapton, Lauryn Hill, and Nirvana—all acts who have

9. Never Say Never
10. Pray

Justin says that he wrote the album's single, "Pray," to bring attention to a world in crisis. The music video for the song opens with a montage of people in need.

released "unplugged" albums. On the album, listeners hear the real, unvarnished Justin playing some of his most familiar songs.

Following is a track list from *My Worlds Acoustic:*

1. One Time
2. Baby
3. One Less Lonely Girl
4. Down to Earth
5. U Smile
6. Stuck in the Moment
7. Favorite Girl (Live)
8. That Should Be Me

For those who have followed his charitable contributions, it's a topic close to his heart.

"It's a very uplifting song, very motivational. It definitely comes from the heart," he told Ryan Seacrest in a radio interview. "I wrote 'Pray' thinking I wanted to help others and I feel like I have a responsibility to do so," Justin said in a press release.

was crazy. Barbra Streisand was on one side of me and Celine Dion was on the other side of me and I felt like, 'This is so big.'"

And it was big. The 25th anniversary version of the song brought much-needed and immediate relief to Haiti.

Drawing on Jackson and others as inspiration, Justin decided to go big on his *My World* tour. For every ticket sold, he donates $1 to Pencils of Promise, an organization dedicated to promoting education worldwide.

Founded in 2008 by Adam Braun, the organization has mobilized efforts and raised funds to provide educational materials and build schools across the world in areas where resources are sorely needed.

"There are more than 75 million children without access to education," the group's website explains. Pencils of Promise's goal is no modest one. They are "creating a movement of people who [see] themselves as global citizens, regardless of age or status."

Pencils of Promise has already built 20 schools in Asia and Central America. Justin's goal is to help raise enough money to build 100. "It adds up fast," Justin wrote in *First Step 2 Forever*. "[With proceeds from] the second leg of the tour alone, we're building 15 schools around the world."

However, Pencils of Promise is only one of a number of charities to which Justin has donated his time and effort. He participated in the Clinton Global Initiative Event, established by former president Bill Clinton to examine major global problems. He supports PETA

and recently appeared in an advertisement to promote the adoption of shelter pets. He has joined the It Gets Better campaign against teen bullying. He's also performed for Idol Gives Back (to benefit health organizations for children worldwide), the Canada for Haiti Telethon, and SOS Saving Ourselves: Help for Haiti, and appeared on a recent episode of ABC's philanthropy series *Extreme Makeover: Home Edition*.

"It's about helping people out that haven't had opportunity," Justin told CNN about his charity efforts. "I'm inspired by children and other kids…. Charities that involve kids are…important to me."

And that's no lip service. A portion of his CD sales for *My Worlds Acoustic* benefit the Children's Miracle Network,

with its children at his concerts. "It's just crazy that I'm a wish," he told CNN.

Justin was honored in 2010 with

He is also heavily involved with the Make-A-Wish foundation. "It's just crazy that I'm a wish," he told CNN.

a charity that raises funds for over 170 children's hospitals across the country.

He has been generous with both his money and time. He is also heavily involved with the Make-A-Wish Foundation, an organization that grants wishes to children who have life-threatening medical conditions. He regularly visits

Variety's Power of Youth Philanthropy Award at the publication's fourth annual ceremony for his contributions to Pencils of Promise, among other organizations. The magazine's event recognizes efforts toward charitable causes and promotes philanthropy among young people.

EXTRA! EXTRA!:
Justin Gets Clipped

It was the snip heard 'round the world. On Monday, February 21, 2011, just a week shy of his 17th birthday, Justin did what many fans thought was the unthinkable: he cut his signature 'do.

It all started with a little teaser he wrote on Twitter that morning: "thinking about getting a haircut....hmmmmmm." But as the Bieber loyal know all too well, the singer is notorious for his practical jokes.

It's not uncommon to see Justin turn up in a clever disguise (like the time he showed up in Coke-bottle glasses and a nifty old-fashioned mustache for the 2011 Critics Choice Awards press line). He also

caused a furor at a November 2010 book signing for his autobiography when he showed up to the event with a new look. As it turned out, he just parted it on the opposite side. (Phew!) Clipping those locks on the other hand? That's a different story altogether.

He'd been coy about the issue in the press, dodging interviewers' questions. One day he'd hint that a cut was coming, the next he'd say that it'd never happen. In December 2010 he told Barbara Walters, "I think after my movie I might cut my hair a little shorter." Then Beliebers breathed a sigh of relief in January 2011 when he told Matt Lauer, "I am not shaving it off" but instead was having fun "just messing it up a lot."